DIMINUENDO

Katrinka Moore

Diminuendo by Katrinka Moore
ISBN:978-1-949790-66-5
eISBN: 978-1-949790-67-2
Copyright © 2022 Katrinka Moore. All rights reserved.

Cover art: Katrinka Moore
Copy editor: Cindy Hochman of "100 Proof" Copyediting Services
Layout and book design by Mark Givens

First Pelekinesis Printing 2022

For information:
Pelekinesis, 112 Harvard Ave #65, Claremont, CA 91711 USA

Library of Congress Cataloging-in-Publication Data

Names: Moore, Katrinka, author.
Title: Diminuendo / Katrinka Moore.
Identifiers: LCCN 2022001118 (print) | LCCN 2022001119 (ebook) | ISBN
   9781949790665 (paperback) | ISBN 9781949790672 (epub)
Subjects: LCGFT: Poetry.
Classification: LCC PS3613.O56297 D56 2022 (print) | LCC PS3613.O56297
   (ebook) | DDC 811/.6--dc23/eng/20220111
LC record available at https://lccn.loc.gov/2022001118
LC ebook record available at https://lccn.loc.gov/2022001119

www.pelekinesis.com

Diminuendo

KATRINKA MOORE

in memory of Robin, radiant

Contents

Weave of the World

Upon Waking	11
Pluck	12
Coming to Light	13
Adagio	14
Field Work	16
Sensei	17
Still	18
Marginal	19
Light Matter	20
For shining air is made of many particles	21
Scatterhoard	22
Distance	23
Thin Places	24
Night Road	26
Visit	27
Reprieve	28
So open and yet so secret	29
Sojourner	30

Diminuendo

Threnody	35
Source	37
Trespass	38
Kite	40
Diminuendo	41
Ash	42
Sapling	43
Gale	44

Feathered Serpent	45
Wayward	46
Why is there so much beauty	47
Delight in Discord	48
No light but rather darkness visible	49
Bare	50
Disquiet	51
Absconder	52
Tale	53

Refugia

Visiting the Hermit Not Finding Her	57
Shelter	58
Song	59
Rising	60
Night Flight	61
The Grammar of Animacy	62
Familiars	63
Unbridled	64
Counterpoint	65
Late	66
Descant	67
Outliers	68
Refugia	69
Meantime	70
Notes	72
Acknowledgments	74

Weave of the World

Upon Waking

Some spirited particles take wing
won't come back   can't

no matter how we sing out   cry

Others try to make up the absence
but miss the ones that have gone

Drawn into the dew   the air   they call back
were always with us   as it turns out   entangled

so the wrenching has a purpose
dissolves a boundary that isn't there

Heartened   I'm here   intact   lie
beside my love   who's still asleep
inside   his own particles   outside

Lovely in its way   this pulse
behind the left ear whispering   *finity*
whisper so thin it's invisible
strong as a spiderweb   We're
all caught in it like moths

Pluck

Comes from a long line
of thieves   steals moments
sun warm on her back   takes

her own time   Whole days
plundered in pursuit of nothing much
Air circles   fluff and feathers float

Cadged hours   overdue   returned
wrinkled smudged torn

Dust-up   bandit bounds
through the tall grass   she's lifted
the shadow from the sundial

Coming to Light

As if your mind were a house
        and wind blew in
        flung open windows
        winnowed
        cast away thoughts
as if chance could clear

As if the world were a restless swarming
        always coming to light
        and disappearing
as if it were made   not of things
        but relations

As if   lost   you kept walking
        stopping to listen
        stumbling on
as if a glimpse were enough
as if stillness

Adagio

even the things that are most "thinglike"
are nothing more than long events

These few acres   once
a homestead   once
ancient forest   once
scraped clear by ice-
dragged stone

Not being   but becoming   Each
boulder   an adagio of dust

A stand of second growth and waving
fields of goldenrod cradle
the little house   Nothing
between us and wild yonder
but a few sheltering gases

The darkness out there   not
the emptiness we sense   but
an entity   its own waving field

Afternoon fades   distinctions
diminish   What's animate
inanimate   Most of us slide
into silence   Crickets
chant   cattails tap one another

languages overlap   An acorn sprout
launches through decaying
layers of leaves   I shuffle
words   Beneath the trees
roots interlace

Field Work

Her mind a passerine
claws firm on the bough

her body a flowering
tree   She knows

what's blooming
A luminist

she sees light
fall into woods

waft over
the undergrowth

A numinist
she reflects

the weave of seen
and unseen

What's in her field box

A spectrum   spirit
tin   spyglass

mud-splattered
map of air

Sensei

Finally the milkweeds split
and silk-winged seeds slow-
stream   breeze-borne

A few come to ground   burrow
doze until spring

*Who can remain still
until the moment of action*

Hesitation   an idea
in shadow   patience
of a tree   a boulder

Light   in its own time
falls and fills   fills
and trembles at the edges

How did Sensei teach
us   novices   to dance
I think she said   *wait*

Still

Rain clearly coming   storm
but I stay   stand on a boulder

in the stream-split field   Savor
cool wind   afternoon of a hot

still day   Watch ash-colored
clouds swarm over South Mountain

Test the limits of time   space
All possible states   hover

Marginal

Ice pond   watery
crown   I skip stones

    splatter reflections
    of bankside pines

    scoot across sprouting
    cracks in the crust

Come spring the stones sink
to the bottom

Threshold and the space
on either side

What's weighty   what's
insignificant

Margin   *feather on the edge
of a bird's wing*

The way meaning travels
from *border* to *marker*
to *not worthy of notice*

Latin *margo*   The quarry
of a hawk is a mark

Light   Matter

Mutable border   mud and muck
cattails sidle into shallows

The open water always the color
of sky   catches a jay flying
over   trackless   feathery

Shoreline willow dives
below ripples   cat's paw

Surface that swallows sun
and moon

A heron glides down to fish
at the edges   Her image
swims up to meet her

For shining air is made of many particles

What is this humming
field

    Purr and shimmy   bee
    and aster

As presence offers pure
attention

attention hallows feast
and frolic

This sweep of land transcends
the turning

of the year   stays numinous
when hum has gone

Scatterhoard

How to find   things
hidden
                  Songbirds
cache seeds   retrieve
by landmarks   thwart
thieves

Not every thought can be
unknotted   the rush
of the whole
                A flock
of leaves   skirrs
across the clearing

To crack open   a kernel
of quiet
            empty circle
from which all things
radiate

Salted away   in veins
in marrow   a deep-seated
yen   for far-flung sky
steppe   savannah   fen

Distance

A blustery headland   cluster
of boulders   remnant of henge
or burial ground   yet when
we step between the stones   we find
a hearth of recent use   Sunlight
spills in   the gusts cut off

Below   the unheard waves recast
the shoreline ancient people knew

We venture down the rugged
path   skirt a marsh   scale
grassy dunes   Feel thrum
of breakers   burn of wind
Descend into distance
ocean   sky

Thin Places

It's far from here   where
my ancestors tended sheep
and cattle   waited for rain

but I make my way out   when
I can   The *fetch of space*
unbounded scope   Beyondness

I carry with me   myself
a fleck in the landscape
swaddled in dry   still   air

as I stand on the once-ocean
floor   waves of sandstone   tide
forever coming in

lift my eyes toward the sky islands
linger on a lone creosote bush
growing in rock cliff

For a moment   a limb
of yellow flowers   sways
on ancient sea wind

In the jumble of peaks
and ridges   floating above
the coastless desert   open to the sun

I take refuge in a thicket of juniper
dark and close   What's shadow
what's substance

For a moment   prickly leaves
part   let in light
from a sister world

Overhead   a hawk spirals
toward high cirrus streams
themselves a scrim   one

of those thin places   She
flashes a bright underwing
flies through

Night Road

Ghost birds cry   flash
in the headlights   dogleg

to skim swells of timothy
on either side

Flight-calls sail   tumble
through wide open windows

Spell between the old
moon and the new

Milky Way burns against
blackness   almost brightens

the road   which now snakes
downhill   into

a hollow   follows
a dark-tuned stream

Visit

Deer path   stir and snap   splashes
of sunlight scoot across trunks

Forest-combing   we garner pine cone
scales   acorn caps   chanterelle

She comes into the cabin   little smile
on her face   notes and scraps   dusty sill

settles on the daybed   I'd tidied a bit
rolled up wrinkled packing paper

She tears off a piece   sketches
clouds in the creases

    ancestor painting a stag
    from a curve on a cave wall

Grey-blue storm swells   tint
of petrichor   brush of thunder

She adds a strip of birch bark
from our gleaning   boat

or home in the tempest

Reprieve

When the waters recede the kitchen's
open to the sky   suddenly blue in clear
warm autumn   We can see our shadows
after a long time without them

A mockingbird perched on an unroofed beam
whistles phrase after phrase   above
the peeling wallpaper   For now

the river flows within its banks
I call to the light   *stay*

So open and yet so secret

Earth and her uncountable
entities   with their own
ways of being   blend
This world-wide breathing
this humming   Awash
in awareness   waves
in a sea of perceiving

You guide a canoe   landfall
uncertain   navigate furrows
and currents   See the nomadic
stars   Living   listening

Sojourner

Tiny white asters   blossom
on leafy long stems   Some wonders
happen over and over   Thunder
month   Last night the storm clouds
vanished   the Big Dipper sparkled
above the trees   Sometimes a rarity
rolls in   sizzles as it passes the sun

Yellow moth skims the flowers   I sidled
through the dark   eyes on the ground
flashlight   Wild   they come up
wherever they please   Stay a little
Doused the torch   looked up   Below
the Pointer Stars   its luminous head
tail blown back by solar wind

Motionless morning air   Ancient
as earth   faster   frozen in space
Some say   portent of calamity
weave of the world unraveling
A scanty breeze   the star-blooms
glimmer   Some see   a harbinger
of hope   mending brokenness
before it sails to the cold far reaches

Diminuendo

Threnody

when all was still ahead
and shimmering
   drunken summer bees
   lost in her hair
   darting off like dreams

you sang
that halting song
the beautiful   broken
gone long-gone
   let me hold out my hands

sea of stars in the heavens
the heavens in glimmering seas
crescent moons on their backs
babies in deep black sky
boats on the water like bones

winter's chant cajoling her northward
necklace of islands on a dark lake
   awake on moonless nights
     ice thunder and boom

ghost voices
in the blink
of my ancient eye

dearheart   truant   orbiting
hailstorm   swims away
to the place where
her becoming began

Source

Live oak and Spanish
moss once spanned
the creek-crossed lowland

The woods razed
years ago   now turned
to grass   tractable

I know the way back
bone-deep   eyes closed
know the land's being

despite the breach
where trees once fed
on light   What's left

eclipses   absence
embraces the rift

Trespass

Deep in the woods
a wounded owl
sunlight flickering
over the ground
A boy with a gun
hears a girl's

step   hears the girl's
heartbeat   deep in the woods
The boy with a gun
and the wounded owl
stand on the ground
sunlight flickering

under the oaks   flickers
over the girl
over the ground
shimmers the woods
shimmers the owl
The boy with a gun

holds onto his gun
eyes darting   eyes flicker
away from the owl
away from the girl
too late to the woods
too late to the shimmering ground

this trespassed-on ground
The boy with his gun
stole into the woods
heart beating   sun flickering
Too-late-to-come girl
the once-flying owl

The wounded owl
stands on the ground
looks at the girl
at the boy with his gun
Afternoon flickering
deep in the woods

Kite

Lifts   hitched to earth
       angles toward high
            winds   the sun

Sends sparks
      down the long
           leash of string

Ballast and sail signal
      each other   parley
          unspool   reel in

Currents shift   kite
      plunges   tussles
          with a leafy sycamore

How to untangle
      mend splits and gashes
          tape tatters together

Fetched inside   it's restless
      twitches   pines
          for open sky

Diminuendo

Above our sleep   thousands
migrate   through once-dark
skies   Chirp and tseet
to keep together   keep
on course   to keep
from vanishing

Here below   aloneness
looms   Whispers stir
crescendo through
the wood   whisk limbs
aside   to reach the edge
of open   where a sole crow
flies   without a caw   Each
wing-beat   shears the air

Ash

Slow-dying ash   still mostly
thick and green   though now
some leaves are yellowing

The high bare limbs   a haunt
of choice for goldfinches   who
facing east   warble as the sun

appears   deep-red sphere
crossing the sky shrouded
in haze   Come night

the stars and even Jupiter
are dim   Three thousand
miles away wildfires

rage   Here   bright singing
birds   the glow of early
color-shifting   fall

Sapling

She's feckless   sometimes
drifts   sometimes careens
seldom relinquishes hope

Mind full of birds   antsy
indoors   wants space
to flail her limbs   In love

with light and motion   Un-
easy in company   itches
to be gone   Stirs

the air   whips up
a wind   trees sway
every which way

Gale

Glint of feather
                night crow cawing

     What's that swaying   shard of light

    Slender lindens   reel
      A seasoned spruce   uproots
         keels over

Sparks shout out
                beyond the water

          See her braids   swing at her back

A sunny place that waves and curves
      like space   then veers

                   What's that flapping
                   that dark sound

Well-worn foot trails   falter
                    fade to nothing

     I try
          but there's no crossing over

She can't hear me

Feathered Serpent

coils around me   scale
and pinion   unwinds
releases   beckons me
upward   We climb
switchback and spiral

She gains the peak   glides
into air   I follow   float
above the outstretched
world   Don't see
my guide withdraw
her task complete

I sink to earth   find
soft brown clay to mold
my neverborn   who rises
radiant   skims mountain
summits   sails on skywind
soars   beyond the sun

Wayward

ones who live outside   thunder
lightning   sunshine   They listen
neither direct   nor intervene   A few

spells might have some effect
but mostly what they practice
is attentiveness   Undaunted

that their lore's unheeded   they
carry on   Unwicked sisters who
refute the role of augury   contend

that stars and birds have no concern
with human want   Refute the thought
that thought is high and other ways

of living low   *The passed-down story
that echoes in your mind*   they say
you cherish it   too dearly

Why is there so much beauty

What keeps us   earth   life
handful of sweet notes   hidden
thrush   glint of lowering
sun   a rain-brushed stone

Slow-moving calamity
quickens   flourishes

Hieroglyphs on scraps of molted
bark   Bones of warriors

*This is not our world
with trees in it*   Latecomers
we believe it was all made
for us   misunderstand
the nature of give and take   Unwilling
to relinquish our hold

A scourge spreads   Buried
dread a dream calls up

It's not quite a song   the same
few notes   over and over

Delight in Discord

I'll have a starling

What a clamor   this twilight chorus
staged in a ginkgo   almost leafless
dark birds that meld with dusky branches
a rowdy crowd   a murmuration
murmur as *complain   accuse*   I hear

voices full of spunk   delight
in discord   chatter   whistle   purr
that rises into rattle   boisterous
brash as Hotspur's rants   his taunts
cavils for the sport of squabble

No light   but rather darkness visible

No turning back   belongings left
behind   rubble   wind-stirred dust

Steel fragments glisten   blood-red
wildflowers holler   Ravaged terrain
fireblown   hollowed as bones

Some on the watch to spread
pandemonium   Their dark purpose
begins as skirmish   becomes debacle

Others long to escape   into air
unearth   uncharted sanctuary

A few souls stand in defiance
edge of a cliff   throw stones

A single shot   aghast   sweet
scent of milkweed

Bare

A wind like this
cold   acrobatic
lays us all bare
nurtures breaches

Cold   acrobatic
it rifts and rends
nurtures breaches
whittles at our edges

our rifts and rents
How to weather it
whistle at the edges
turn our backs

howl   Whether we
tack   zigzag
turn our backs
there's no eluding

its zigzagged attack
lays us all bare
No eluding
a wind like this

Disquiet

The saga's recast   each
unfolding day

Decrees declared   withdrawn
New edicts shift the ground

beneath us   Hiatus
turns to disarray

Sparseness   spareness
scaling back   Unpeopled

houses   loss after loss
Disturbances that thrive

within catastrophe   All
angles   sharp points

utterly silent   poised
to strike

Absconder

When I was a child
I slept in a room
whose windows opened onto woods
Dawn birds darted
in sunglow between
trees   calling   calling

Heat lightning on the horizon
rain never falls

We set out early   decamp
slip away   desert
ride hard   ford a river
unbridle the horses   who
graze   small   slow   steps

Like any animal I live
with my own need   and
that of others   how
they rub together
your hunger   mine

Tale

Told in sweeping tones   as if viewed
from the stars

Litany of conflicts   victories   dominion
Schemes that yield the unforeseen

Foreboding gleams   in pauses   between
words

As in many stories   a hero
reaches too far

gains power   loses
the way

Endless   hungry   rushing
river

Sources of darkness   stalk
the margins

Refugia

Visiting the Hermit   Not Finding Her

Chaparral ridge
Where the trail fades

I follow a dry ravine
down to a shallow river

a cottonwood
her mud-brick hut

She's not at home   I lean
against the tree

    Chickadees dart
    between the leaves

    the current glides above
    smooth white stones

She's out   somewhere
gathering sage

I sit under the cottonwood
The sun rolls over the ridge

Shelter

Uncertainty's our home
now   as it always was

The trail's unmade   a few
cairns remain

Notched bones
unreadable

Tracks too cold
to follow

A spell of seclusion
a sort of sanctuary

Relieved of the need
to be heard or seen

I study mystery and beauty
in the midst of sorrow

and suffering   Mind
water   wind   stone

Song

Begins with a clear pour   then tumbles
a string of small bells   spilling
It's over quick   and the span between
riffs is uneven   moments   days

Sometimes   an echoer pipes up
from another tree   in another part
of the forest   Amateur birder
I've never seen the singer   though
I whisper to myself   *hermit thrush*

Amateur hermit   content   restless
lifting my chin   somehow   to listen
Leaves rustle   a whiff of air tosses
down drops   yesterday evening's rain

Rising

I wake in the night   the ridge
across the valley glows   An out-
sized crescent climbs above
the mountains   A small

grey cloud rolls in and hides
the light   By chance
I rose right at that moment
stumbled on so brief

a scene   The Taoists say
to take delight   abandon
thoughts of holding

Night Flight

One of many   a feather on a wing
      a flock of wings   whistling
A scaup in the skein   feels shift   shifts
      herself   Steering by stars
deep memory of flyway   of waterscapes
      where waterfowl   scatter
dive to forage   tuck beaks in back feathers
      sleep as they float   Come dusk
a few ducks lift into air   circle   Others
      lift and circle   until   all
alight   Moored below   dreaming awake
      I call up   ancestral paths
      cold high air   wild wholeness

The Grammar of Animacy

A red-tailed hawk glides overhead
shadow grazing wild thyme   Who's
in ki's talons   vole   mouse
    What is this *ki*

        Rooted in ancient
        language

   to signify a being of the living earth

From the edge of the forest
a whistle-cry

    Who is a *being*
    Oak   fox   cloud   boulder   song

       Words breathe   cross
       borders   shift

    A loan word   drawn
    from the Potawatomi

Two hawks sky-spiral
swoop   swerve
spin-as-one

    Let's call the plural   *kin*
    come down from old English

We say buteo   raptor   bird
of prey   The red-tails know
kin's own true name

    Ki calls to ki   *keee*

Familiars

Kinship of leaf and
feather   the spine
the veins   the way

they're both devoted
to the whole   know
when the time to part

has come   Airy
deft at spinning off
Sometimes they spiral

slowly   down   sometimes
wind-ride   far from home
until   earth-caught

they light upon
their shadows

Unbridled

Wind gallops up the mountain
sunlit morning   barrels
into forest   Flash and
shadow sweep and splash
with every gust   with each
resounding surge

Limbs and boughs thump
down   Skinny saplings
pitch   rebound   Full-leafed
branches   fluster   flail
Pine spires careen   Wildwood's
inner life   spills open

Counterpoint

He's light as feathers
                          If the body came into being

but when he lights on the yet-to-flower
goldenrod
                          because of spirit

the tall soft stem curves down
to the ground
                          that is a marvel

He hangs on   rides the arching
over
                          but if spirit came into being

then flies to a sky-high limb
                          because of the body

sings a phrase over and over
                          that is a marvel of marvels

Late

Autumn's brilliant burst scales
back to rusty glow   to empty
branches   Sunlight seeks out

secrets in the forest   Night
falls quickly   Red-rising
Mars sails the southern

arc   trails Jupiter and Saturn
We live in the sky   cling
to Earth's skin   turn away

from the vastness   always
racing toward unbeing   This
moment   hurled headlong

between deep-rooted trees
shorn limbs stretching
starward   cold dark

before dawn   one   then
another   meteor

Descant

Gathers the drift of life
    constellations
of moments   sensations

Unravels this-then-that
    knits
reflection   reverie

Sings of all being
    breathtaking
in the unmaking

Outliers

As the ice receded
a few seeds migrated

north   Stowed in bird
beaks   and in the hairs

of mammals   storm-riding
they abandoned home

vaulted to bareness   nestled
into the crust   took root

As the ice recedes   tales
of wanderlust   exile

A few seeds migrate
north   leave forest

behind   its fate to fade
in the seething

Refugia

The weathered world   frays
splinters

Strewn skeletons   raw soil   rusty
artifacts

Scanty remnants   flora
fauna

scatter across the face
of the earth

retreat   adapt   persist

Is this story a running
river   or the sea   tides
that swell   retract   return

Unlikely gatherings   small bevies
of sundry beings

come to live   in an in
between

An unworded dialect   emerges
that all divine

Meantime

Who knows what people believe
Uncertain landscapes shift

overlap   Relics of a past
that may not have happened

I think we're in a meantime   neither
beginning nor end

Between earth and sky   ever-
cycling despair and hope

That porous border where
self touches outside

wild like a full-leaved tree
grown from a seed   lucky

to have landed
in an auspicious site   lucky

in the weather
the sunlight

Notes

"Coming to Light": The phrases "restless swarming" and "coming to light" are from Carlo Rovelli's *Seven Brief Lessons on Physics*, tr. Erica Segre and Simon Carnell.

"Adagio": The epigraph is from Carlo Rovelli's *The Order of Time*, tr. Erica Segre and Simon Carnell.

"Sensei" is for Mariko Sanjo. The third stanza is from Lao-Tzu's *Tao te Ching*, tr. Gia-Fu Feng and Jane English.

"*For shining air is made of many particles*": The title is from Lucretius' *The Nature of Things*, tr. A.E. Stallings.

"Thin Places": The phrase *fetch of space* is from Robert Macfarlane's *Underland*.

"Visit" is for Robin Glassman.

"*So open and yet so secret*": The title is from Nan Shepherd's *The Living Mountain*.

"Threnody" is a cento with lines from Holly Anderson's *The Night She Slept With a Bear*.

"Why is there so much beauty": The title is a question posed by Manu Prakash, quoted by James Gorman in *The New York Times*. The italicized sentence in the fifth stanza is from Richard Powers' *The Overstory*.

"Delight in Discord": The epigraph is from *Henry IV, Part 1*.

"No light but rather darkness visible": The title is from *Paradise Lost*.

"The Grammar of Animacy": Italics are from Robin Wall Kimmerer's "Speaking of Nature" in *Orion Magazine*, June 2017.

"Counterpoint": Italics are words attributed to Jesus in the *Gospel of Thomas*, tr. Marvin Meyer and Elaine Pagels.

"Refugia": Refugia are safe havens for biodiversity under changing environmental conditions.

Acknowledgments

Grateful acknowledgment is made to the following publications in which these poems, sometimes in earlier versions, first appeared:

Civilization in Crisis anthology: "No light   but rather darkness visible"
Cold Mountain Review: "Why is there so much beauty," "Shelter"
Downtown Brooklyn: A Journal of Writing: "Outliers"
Exposition Review: "Meantime"
Feral: A Journal of Poetry and Art: "Gale"
First Literary Review-East: "Pluck," "Sapling," "Feathered Serpent," "Delight in Discord," "Unbridled"
Gyroscope Review: "The Grammar of Animacy"
Hole in the Head Review: "Upon Waking," "Counterpoint"
Leaping Clear: "Visiting the Hermit   Not Finding Her"
Otoliths: "Sensei," "Threnody"
SWWIM: "Field Work"
Terrain: "Adagio," "Marginal," "Distance," "Visit," "Disquiet," "Absconder," "Tale," "Descant"
The New Verse News: "Ash"
The Stillwater Review: "Diminuendo," "Rising," "Still," "Reprieve," "Song"
Wild Roof: "Coming to Light," "So open and yet so secret"

Many thanks to Caroline Beasley-Baker and Maura Candela for their insightful manuscript readings. I'm very grateful to the One O'clock Poets and the Evergreen Poets for their astute comments on many of the poems. Thanks also to Kathleen B. Jones and Katherine Catmull. Deep appreciation to Mark Givens of Pelekinesis for his generosity and support. Undying love to Michael and gratitude for his music, physics, and encouragement.

112 Harvard Ave #65
Claremont, CA 91711 USA

pelekinesis@gmail.com
www.pelekinesis.com

Pelekinesis titles are available through Small Press Distribution, Baker & Taylor, Ingram, Bertrams, and directly from the publisher's website.

www.ingramcontent.com/pod-product-compliance
Lightning Source LLC
Chambersburg PA
CBHW050821090426
42737CB00022B/3466